Disclaimer: This book is fiction *of Oz* and *Alice in Wonderland* are fiction, and so is this book. Only Butch & Louie are real—and of course, the Harleys are too. However, unlike *The Wizard of Oz* and *Alice in Wonderland* this is an adult book. It's not a book for children, so don't let your children buy it, much less read it. Reading it could cause lasting nightmares or trauma. Butch & Louie aren't responsible for your kids. Let them read *The Wizard of Oz, Alice in Wonderland,* or some other kids' book that survives cancel culture. If you still aren't getting it, please refer to the Acknowledgments, Dedication, Introduction, Accolades, Prologue, Epigraph, Forward, and Preface page below for clarification.

butchandlouie@hotmail.com

Vol. 1 HR Bad Boy Humor ISBN 978-1-7370552-0-4
Vol. 1 E-book ISBN 978-1-7370552-1-1
Vol. 0 Intro to Bad Boy Humor ISBN 978-1-7370552-2-8

First paperback edition April 2021

Edited by Butch & Louie
Cover art by Butch & Louie
Artwork by Butch & Louie

Butch & Louie Publishing
Copyright

All rights reserved. No part of this book may be reproduced or used in any manner without the prior written permission of the copyright owner, except for the use of brief quotations in a book review.

Acknowledgments
Dedication Page
Introduction
Accolades
Prologue
Epigraph
Forward
Preface

Yo, bite us!

Table of Contents

Give Me French Fries	5
Faux Jumelles	7
That's a Small i	10
It's Just Plain Stifling	11
Friction Burns	14
But They're Cute	16
Sexting	17
Suck It Up	19
Sandwiches	21
Looking For Love	23
Define Me	25
Space for Guests	27
They Ain't Diet Cookies	28
Pepe Le Pew	30
Cha-Ching	32
Baby Makes Three	33
Tiny Bubbles	35
Ouch!	38
Grrrr	39
Cat Nip	41
Shit Farm	43
Firewood	46
Big Brother	47
Cancel Me Now	71
Green Eggs and Ham	73
Eyewitness Testimony	75
French Is in the Air	76
I Philia	77
My Best Side	78
My Best Side Part 2	82
It's Cold Outside	85
Stay for Dinner	87
Walk in My Shoes	88
Call of Nature	89
Chew Toys	91
A Better World Through Plastics	93
Curbside Service	95
A Different Cord	97
Somebody's Got to Do It	98
Turn Out the Lights	99
It Ain't Over Till It's Over	101
Look It Up	102
Very Complex	104
Lock Them Up	107
Clothing Optional	110
Index	114
Butch & Louie Bio	115

Saddle Up!
It's time to ride with
Butch & Louie.

Give Me French Fries

When we were kids, Mr. Potato Head was one of our favorite toys. What the hell is up with Hasbro now? In late February, Hasbro said it was dropping the "Mr." in front of its Mr. Potato Head toy, which has been around since 1952. Hasbro executives said they wanted to make the toy more inclusive by removing the "Mr." However, we suspect there are other motives behind the move.

- There were too many complaints that Mr. Potato Head looked like your father.

- Hasbro hopes Idaho potato farmers will finally forgive them for replacing the real potato with a plastic one.

- Dropping the Mr. sounded like a better idea than adding tattoos, and a nose ring.

- Hasbro really hated their 4.7 rating on Amazon.

- The company plans to hold a "guess which parts are missing" contest before releasing the new potato head toy.

- Now, kids are free to use sweet potatoes.

- Hasbro's CEO was jealous of the Super Spud nickname.

- Hasbro didn't think through the implications this would have for Mr. Rogers. "Won't you be my neighbor?" Not anymore!

- Hasbro has a bunch of new Mr. Potato Heads in inventory and is going to sell them as used on eBay when the price goes up.

- It's a lot cheaper to make one gender-less Potato Head than a Mr. and Mrs. Potato Head.

Faux Jumelles

Thinking about getting a new pair of breasts? A lot of women are, so cosmetic surgery is big business. Remodeling anything requires skill in selecting materials and a vision of the before and after. Since we're experts in all kinds of breasts, here's a little training course to get you started right.

Materials are a top priority, so knowing the difference between things like silicone and silicon is important. Silicone is a synthetic polymer made of siloxanes. So, silicone is essentially rubber. Uses for it include adhesives, lubricants, cooking utensils, electrical insulation and since 1962, breasts.

Silicon, on the other hand, is a naturally occurring element used to make semiconductors for computers, phones and other electrical equipment. And, there's a California valley named after it. Silicon is rarely used in cosmetic surgery, at least so far.

Saline is another option for implants. It's simply salt water. Put $10 worth of saline in plastic bags and after a little medical magic, you have $5000 breasts. It sounds easy, but experts say you shouldn't try this at home.

Silicone and saline implants feel substantially different. Saline implants are harder and good for playing rugby, but they tend to have ripples. Silicone implants feel much softer and smoother, but silicone isn't as safe as saline according to trial attorneys.

Of course, implants come in different sizes. A woman can go from an A cup all the way to Dolly Parton. However, busting out from an A to a Dolly in one surgery is going to generate a lot of water cooler talk at the office, so get ready for some tricky explaining.

Your implant specialist, the surgeon, will call the procedure breast augmentation. It's all about the money. Augmentation sounds way more expensive , than saying, "We're going to fill your tits with caulk."

After the surgery, each breast comes with a label that has the size and care instructions on it. Of course, the label has a DO NOT TOUCH FOR 2 WEEKS warning on it because of the swelling. Additionally, the stitches need time to heal (unless a zipper was put in.) and your partner might get too aggressive unwrapping the surprise package. The first pair of breasts usually lasts about 10 years before the surgeon needs money and suggests replacing them.

As you might expect, breast research attracts a lot of interest. Recent innovations include the gummy bear implant, which is a teardrop-shaped gel implant. While it holds its shape better than the other implants, every time your partner wants a snack, they start looking at your tits like they're PEZ dispensers.

Another option is the fat injection procedure. Harvested fat is injected into the breasts to enlarge them. While this sounds like a more natural approach, over time the breasts tend to become lumpy. For those who want the XL augmentation, removing too much fat from one spot leaves a crater that needs filling in with Bondo, and, of course, that's an upcharge.

To beat the high cost of surgery, some buyers are heading to Mexico. However, this kind of medical tourism is not problem free. Patients have noticed that mariachi music causes their breasts to vibrate, and a few clinics are using recycled window insulation, which makes the new breasts unseasonably warm.

Like everything medical, implant surgery attracts malpractice claims. A recent one involved a surgeon who used silicon instead of silicone implants. (It's easy to grab the wrong box when the spelling is so close.)

The court ordered tests on the breasts, and the results confirmed the silicon augmented breasts were smarter and able to solve more problems than the silicone ones. Rather than implementing new procedures to prevent this from happening again, the Society of Plastic Surgeons recommended that their members charge more for the smarter tits.

That's a Small i

We like iPhones, and luckily, we find quite a few of them. Apple recently introduced the new iPhone 12 Pro Max. and of course, it didn't get cheaper. Buying one with 512gb of storage costs $1400. We're talking big bucks for six little inches. So, what's up with that?

- You didn't have a choice. The government sent your stimulus check to the Apple store.

- You dropped your $1200 older iPhone in a toilet that already had other stuff in it.

- It comes with a picture of Steve Jobs.

- Your landlord said you could skip a couple of months of rent.

- Brenda has one!

- Your selfies just look so good on that OLED screen.

- You only had to work full-time for a month at Burger King.

- You've got a lot of really important phone calls to make.

It's Just Plain Stifling

This is really an odd case our friend, Detective Logan, told us about the other day. In an unusual Covid related death, Linda Peachtree died while shopping at the mall in Minneapolis.

While commenting anonymously, thirty-year veteran detective, Mark Logan, told the Star that Ms. Peachtree appears to have died from asphyxiation.

He said, "Peachtree's friends and relatives told us she was very concerned about catching the virus and took extra precautions to reduce her risk."

Asked for examples, he replied, "Well, she stayed twelve feet away from other people, rather than the normal six feet. And instead of wearing one mask, she had on three when we found her."

Pursing his lips and raising an eyebrow, he said, "I guess the extra protection led to her death. When we removed the last of the three masks, her face had a bluish tint to it, and her lips had those purplish maroon streaks we see on strangled vic's."

"Witnesses told us she appeared to be wobbly and gasping for air when she went down. A couple of people said they thought they heard muffled cries for help, but it was impossible to hear her clearly from 12 feet away."

Reverend Bernice Child said, "Linda was a good woman who not only wanted to protect herself, but she wanted to give others a sense they were safe when talking to her. She always waived and shouted to everyone in the congregation from across the street."

Friction Burns

With coronavirus keeping more people away from the gym, home exercise equipment sales are up. However, not everyone can afford Peloton prices, so the next best thing is pole dancing We have a lot of experience with pole dancers, so here's what we've learned.

1. Put your pole somewhere with six feet of clearance all the way around because new pole dancers often fly off. Removable poles, especially if installed by liberal arts graduates, sometimes detach during use, so landing space is necessary.

2. Experienced pole dancers use almost all of the muscles in the major muscle groups and burn a lot of calories with their moves. New pole dancers use their muscles and burn calories picking their asses up off the floor.

3. Clinging to the pole out of fear won't burn anything except your time, so pull up those leggings and get to twirling.

4. Experienced pole dancers injure themselves a couple of times every three years or so, but new dancers average an injury every twenty minutes. Camera flashes cause a lot of those.

5. Husbands are 78 percent more sympathetic and supportive of their wives who are injured while pole dancing than they are from things like getting a hand stuck in the garbage disposal.

6. Handsprings, twines, and carousel moves take practice and sometimes go wrong, causing injuries. Beginners get hurt just getting on and off the pole.

7. Regardless of their experience, every pole dancer we know is up-to-date on the expensive, fashionable pole dancer outfits.

8. Men also benefit physically from pole dancing, but only when nobody else is home.

9. Don't use hand lotion to protect the skin before getting on the pole. It's a really bad idea.

10. Ninety-eight percent of men agreed that naked pole dancing provides a superior form of exercise for their wives and girlfriends. Yo!

But They're Cute

When we were passing through North Carolina, we were disappointed to find out about the demise of one of our favorite events.

The mayor of Andrews, North Carolina said "This is going to be the last year for the New Year's Eve possum drop. Even though we only do it once a year, we get too many complaints from PETA saying that it's too stressful for the possum." The mayor paused, then continued, "We offered to compromise and drop the possum faster, but they just wouldn't agree."

After more than 20 years of watching the furry little guy ring in the New Year, local folks are upset.

"It's our possum and our town," said Ralph Wait. "We've never lost a possum. We don't even keep'em up late. We send'em home right after midnight—well, after a beer or two past midnight!" he said, laughing.

Jeff Green, the owner of the local garage wanted to know, "Who the hell is PETA anyway? They ain't from around here."

Deputy Chris Plier pointed out, "Catching possums is more dangerous than dropping them. They didn't say nutin' about that."

The locals are considering alternatives. One suggestion was to drop an Armadillo—"cause 'dillo's got a shell." Another idea was to shoot a possum, stuff it and then drop the stuffed one. Almost everyone agreed that PETA wasn't likely to complain about a dead possum drop.

Sexting

Sexting is something we just don't do. It attracts too much unwanted attention, which we have plenty of already. But maybe you've been thinking about sending out a couple of dick-pics. With the growing participation in social media, texting pictures of penises is more popular than ever, but it is controversial.

When asked why he chose to share these particular pictures, Don from Australia said, "I enjoy having a penis, so I thought I would let others enjoy it too!"

Marshawn of France said, "I have nothing to hide, so why not? Let's have some fun."

Richard, an American, said, "It's part of my resume on dating apps. It's like 'what's your favorite color', or other get-to-know-you questions."

Linea of Finland added, "I don't have one to share, but I wish I did!"

As a guide to readers who are thinking about sexting for the first time, here's a list of the pros and cons.

Pros

- It stops all the conversations about the size of your hands.

- It could get you job offers in the porn business.

- It separates you from other guys on dating apps.

- If you die without an ID, it could identify you.

- If you want attention, this is one way to get it

Cons

- There are so many decisions involving make-up, shooting angles, good side-bad side posing and getting the correct zoom.

- It might restart the whole office competition thing again.

- It's really easy to tell if you've photoshopped it.

- You'll always feel the picture could have been just a little bit better.

- It could get you five to ten years in prison with other guys who want to show you pictures of their penises.

Suck It Up!

According to some inside sources, which we can't name, we're on a couple of federal watchlists. We guess that means even the people in DC are waiting for Vol. 2. Since everybody in DC is watching everybody else, we don't really feel special. Sometimes all that watching gets creepy.

    Last Thursday, Mandie returned home after a shopping trip and found her couch cushions on the floor, the bottom cabinet doors open, and some bags in the closet pulled down. Horrified, she called the police because she thought a predator had broken into her home.

    After carefully searching the house, police concluded no one had been inside. One of the officers pointed to her robotic vacuum and asked her what it was. Mandie said, "That's Suzie. She vacuums everyday at 10 a.m."

    The officer picked up Suzie and found strands of cotton fibers and pieces of cushion foam hanging from her sweeper brush. He laughed as he said, "Ma'am, maybe this is your intruder!"

    Mandie smiled at the comment as the officers left. She had found Suzie next to the couch when she had come home. Suzie should have been finishing up the vacuuming or in her charging station. Mandie used the remote to dock Suzie before asking with a sigh, "Suzie, did you do all this?"

After spending an hour trying to find a technical support phone number or address for the Chinese company that had manufactured Suzie, Mandie gave up. She concluded that maybe they didn't want to be found.

Next, Mandie searched the internet to see if any other robot vacuum owners had reported unusual behavior around their homes. She found a few random reports of odd incidents like open boxes or missing thumb drives, but no one pointed to a robotic vacuum as the culprit. A lot of the reports came from residents living near DC.

None of this made sense to Mandie; however, she knew she would never look at Suzie the same way again. "No," she thought, "it can't be." But she was definitely going to share her weird day with her husband, Steve, a senior State Department executive.

Sandwiches

New York City, one of our favorite places, now has vending machines that sell coronavirus test kits. The kits are $149. After swabbing your mouth for saliva, the sample is shipped by FedEx to the lab for testing. It takes two days to get the results.

The Oakland International Airport also has one of the vending machines, and Wellness 4 Humanity, the creator, hopes to have them in all major airports shortly.

While some people may see the availability of vending machine test kits as a positive step, there have been a few issues.

- If you change your mind and hit the refund button, that's a lot of quarters.

- If your test kit gets stuck falling out, it ain't like losing a bag of potato chips.

- There's never a line to buy the test kits. Who's going to stand in line behind someone who thinks they have Covid?

- Two days is a long time to wait in an airport for the test results.

- Great, another reason to get mugged in New York.

Looking for Love in All the Wrong Places

We like animals. We try very hard not to run over any when we're riding across the country. We're on PETA's mailing list because they appreciate our efforts to avoid roadkill. Last Thursday, PETA issued a statement saying they were officially recognizing Bigfoot as an endangered species and planned to sponsor programs to protect Bigfoot in the wild.

PETA spokesperson, Ron Sightly, said, "After careful consideration, PETA has decided to get in front of the Bigfoot issue before some nut job actually finds one and either kills it or injures it trying to get a selfie."

PETA's board discussed alternative names for Bigfoot, including Sasquatch or Yeti and their possible misogynist, xenophobic, or homophobic implications. One objection to keeping the Bigfoot name involved local drug dealers that used Bigfoot as their street name. Some worried local kids might wonder why PETA labeled Bigfoot as an endangered species when most of the dealers had a permit to carry a 9 mm without a serial number.

Other board members felt that outside of Baltimore, Chicago, and Detroit, the risk of confusion was low because most kids got their drugs from pizza delivery people, ice cream truck drivers or their mother's purse. In the end, they decided to stick with Bigfoot to reduce potential spelling errors on protest signs made by Gen Z college graduates.

After settling the Bigfoot issue, discussion of the Loch Ness Monster was put on hold until later in the year.

Define Me

The second fastest growing profession in the US is life coaching. A life coach teaches a client how to reach previously unreachable goals. Since, we're sort of life coaches (and role models), we get the life coaching thing really well. We've helped clients reach previously unreachable goals, like paying off debts.

Fortunately, there are no formal qualifications to be a life coach except a strong desire to help others improve themselves for an hourly fee. To better understand how life coaching works, we talked to a few life coaching clients.

Betty from New York told us, "My life coach has helped me get rid of so much stress. I never felt like I had enough time. Then, Omar, my life coach told me, 'Betty, you can't do everything,' and it was like a light bulb went on."

"I started focusing on the things that were important to me like shopping and salon day, and I stopped the unimportant stuff like cleaning the apartment or cooking dinner," Betty explained. "The kids make peanut butter and jelly sandwiches or eat a bowl of cereal when they're hungry."

"My husband, Frank, orders take out when we don't have time to go out for dinner," Betty said.

Asked if there are any downsides to life coaching, Betty said, "Well, Frank really doesn't like Omar or his $300 an hour fee, but Frank is supportive of my need to change, and I only talk to Omar two or three hours a week."

Next, we spoke with Swenton from Los Angeles. He explained, "A month ago, I hired my life coach because I just wasn't going anywhere."

Asked where he wanted to go that he wasn't going, Swenton told us, "I wanted to be part of LA, not just looking in at it. I just didn't know how to do that."

"Mia took me shopping. She helped define me. I leased a Rover, and re-decorated my apartment to look like the new me."

"It wasn't cheap, but it was so worth it. I had to max out a couple of cards, and of course, Mia cost me $5000. She used to be in the escort business. You know, the best don't come cheap!"

Next, we asked Lannie from Louisiana if he had a life coach.

"Yeah, I got a life coach. A few times a week we go to Lafittes and have a few beers. Red tells me everything that's wrong with me, and I tell him he's full of shit. If I want to change something, I'll get off my ass and change it. I don't need an ex-truck driver telling me how to make my life better."

Space for Guests

From time to time, we visit properties listed for sale. It's interesting to see how other people live. Real Estate agents are always looking for a marketing angle to sell a property. When a former Missouri sheriff's 1875 house came on the market, it presented a tricky listing problem. Included with its 2200 square feet of living space were nine jail cells. (We guess the sheriff liked to take his work home.) Here are few catch lines the realtors discussed.

- Works well for a big foster family.

- Unruly neighbor kids, no problem.

- Have you always wanted to help runaways?

- Insist that your new friends stay longer than they planned.

- Finally, a way to keep the kids safe while you rest.

- Husband snore?

- So, your kids want to live in the basement!

They Ain't Diet Cookies

We hang out in Ventura every year waiting for the Girl Scout cookie sales to start. We stuff our saddlebags full of the Samoas and S'mores before we saddle up for our cross country ride. We've found the best way to buy the cookies is to put a sign up on one of the Harley's. We tried, "Hey, little girl," but that didn't work out too well. Now, it looks like we may have to order them online next year.

Since 1917, Girl Scout cookie sales have been an important part of financing troop activities. The original cookie ingredients cost $0.36 for six dozen cookies, and the girls baked them in their moms' kitchens. Scout supporters bought the cookies for $0.35 a dozen, which was six times their cost.

Of course, a lot has changed since then. Because the girls are busier these days playing video games, posting on Instagram and trying to get into the Boy Scouts, they don't have time to bake. Now, thousands of Chinese moms who support scouting activities around the world make the cookies. Even though it's a hard job, a dedicated Chinese mom can bake over 200,000 cookies a year, if she works on them seven days a week 15 hours a day.

In 2014, the Girl Scouts introduced the Digital Cookie platform, which helped young girls make lots of new online friends. In fact, cookie sales to single men who selected the optional personal home delivery have increased by 300 percent.

The Girl Scouts added gluten-free cookies and non-racist cookies to their list of treats in 2020. The discrimination-free cookies are guaranteed to make anyone fat who binge eats a few boxes a day, regardless of their race, ethnicity, or gender.

For 2021, they're considering adding an apolitical cookie that when eaten with a glass of milk blocks all hate thoughts while watching CNN.

The Boy Scouts have always envied Girl Scout cookie sales, and their leadership has occasionally questioned the wisdom of the boys raising woodchucks and making beaver skin hats instead of selling something with sugar in it.

But that may be about to change. It's possible that by 2025, both boys and girls will be part of the same Scout organization with no gender distinction. Scouting focus groups are discussing non-binary cookie names and agender packaging. So far, they haven't talked about woodchucks.

Pepe Le Pew

Sometimes, we go to Europe for special occasions. We hookup with one of the great riding clubs there (like the Bandidos in the UK or No Surrender in Sweden) and do the tourist thing for a few weeks. Here's what we learned about France.

- There are 365 varieties of cheese in France. At least 362 of them taste like shit, so we drink the wine, but we don't eat the cheese.

- The French take a two-hour lunch break every day, and it's illegal to eat lunch at your desk. That's why they have more frequent sex than Americans.

- The French created license plates in 1893. Then, they had to hire cops that could read.

- Thirty-four percent of French residents speak English fluently, but only fifteen percent admit it. Where are those fifteen percent at?

- France has more depressed people than any other country. The most frequently diagnosed reason—tourists.

- In France, it's legal to marry a dead person — because you might have figured out your

- feelings a little too late. In America, you can't marry the dead, but they can vote.

Cha-Ching

We don't use Bitcoin, but it's getting more popular, so we're looking for ways to get some. Here are five things you may not know about Bitcoin.

- Not a single politician, rich guy, civil rights leader, or a dude named Fred has had their picture put on a Bitcoin.

- In 2010, a guy bought two pizzas using 10,000 Bitcoins. Based on the value of a Bitcoin in 2021, those two pizzas cost him $500,000,000. He should have eaten one pizza and kept the other $250,000,000. He must have been single.

- A software bug accidentally created 184 billion Bitcoins. This bug is now the richest bug in the world, and is living anonymously in an unknown thumb drive.

- The DEA says Bitcoins aren't used to buy drugs very often because drug users can't remember their Bitcoin key codes.

- Hookers take Bitcoin, but they don't give change.

Baby Makes Three

We have our own Facebook page. Google "Facebook Butch & Louie," and we're there. But last Thursday we were a little stunned (Yeah, it happens!) by a Facebook post that said 18-year-old Daniellia Oliveri had gotten pregnant by her internet boyfriend, Freddy, through social media contact only.

Their parents were surprised, shocked, and a bit panicked. While Daniellia met Freddy online, the two of them have never met in person, which was confirmed by the parents.

After exchanging texts, Instagram posts, and TikTok videos, they fell in love. Over the next four months, their relationship escalated to Facebook and Skype chats.

Nauseated in the mornings, and not feeling like herself, Daniellia visited her doctor.

Dr. Swande said, "This is a first for me. I did an ultrasound just to check for irregularities, but I never expected to find a fetus. Especially, because Daniellia shows no signs of sexual activity." After pausing, he continued, "Social media is the only possible explanation!'

Bobby Cushy of the CDC's National Vital Statistics Office, which tracks official birth records, said, "Daniellia's news is very exciting to us. We were concerned that with the decline in dating due to cyberspace relationships, it was going to lead to fewer births. So, this is big news!"

Cushy added, "I'll be pleased to fill in the name of the father as Facebook Freddy when the time comes."

Alice Goodsho, an executive with Planned Parenthood, tweeted out, "The opportunities this presents for us are huge."

As teenagers in love, Daniellia and Freddy were both pleased and nervous at the same time. Freddy said, "We'll continue living with our parents for now. It'll be like a gap year, only we're going to raise our baby instead of doing something like eliminating poverty in Brooklyn."

"Yeah," Daniellia said, "I don't see why we can't give our child a normal life using Skype, Zoom and a few apps. I'll be a full-time mom, and Freddy will get a part-time job, so he can afford to Amazon or Instacart over diapers and other baby stuff. I think it will work out fine until we're older, like 28 or so. Then we'll spend time together offline, and maybe even get our own place."

Marsha from Child Services commented, "I guess this will make more parents pay attention to what their kids are doing online."

After thinking about all of this, we've decided to raise our social media interaction age from 15 to menopause and above, just to be safe.

Tiny Bubbles

Everybody's had experience with flatulence (expelling methane) which is a common biological process caused by incomplete food digestion in mammals, including humans. Surprisingly, not much is known about it, even though flatology scientists continue studying it. Here is what they've learned so far.

- Breaking wind is a random event. Despite extensive research, no one has been able to create a model that predicts the occurrence, duration, noise, or side effects of it accurately.

- One characteristic, the odor, is associated with certain diseases like irritable bowel syndrome, lactose intolerance or celiac disease. Many spouses believe they can identify disease related flatulence almost instantly. Some have reported near-death experiences.

- Cows, sheep and termites generate the most methane, but unlike humans, they don't seem to react to it. Scientists expected one or two of them to keel over, or run away from the offenders, but so far, that hasn't happened.

- In the animal world, ferrets are the most surprised and shocked by farting, and so are people on subways and buses.

- Since gas contributes to global warming, Gen Z and Millennials are concerned about it. Cows and sheep have never expressed any global warming anxiety.

- Many climate scientists, and Greta Thunberg, the teenage Swedish climate activist, are worried that flatulence may prevent the world from reaching net zero emissions.

- A termite generates half a micro-gram of methane per day. With billions of termites all over the world, they collectively produce 10 to 20 percent of global green house gas per year. Cars produce 28 percent, so obviously we need electric termites.

- Whales and other sea mammals passing gas may have inspired the 1966 Don Ho song, Tiny Bubbles.

- Despite popular belief, mammal generated methane does not catch on fire. If it did, large herds of cows would be exploding into flames daily.

- To show her commitment to net zero emissions, Greta Thunberg has pledged to never fart again.

- John Kerry's climate plan includes eliminating cows and sheep and telling everybody else to stick a cork in it.

Ouch!

There's a lot of discussion about Covid vaccinations. Some people are for it, and some people are against it. Since we don't wear masks (Well, infrequently!) and we don't social distance, we got our shots. What about you?

    Howard from Encino said, "I'm definitely going to get vaccinated. Posting this on my dating app will be like saying *I'm herpes free.* And I am."

    Stella from Boise said, "I'll pass! This is just another government plan to turn all of us into zombies, so they can control us."

    Chad from Louisiana pointed out, "If everybody else gets it, why do I need it?"

    Marie from Seattle said, "I'm going to get the shot, but it's not really for me. I want to protect everyone around me.?"

Grrrr

Older women dating or marrying younger men is more popular and acceptable, than ever before. These "cougars" are no longer considered desperate women. Now, they're seen as confident, sexy, and desirable due to their life experiences, which their "cubs" appreciate.

We like having relationships with all kinds of women, from one day to maybe five years or so. Our only major constraint is they must be able to stay on the bike regardless of what we're doing, like a high-speed chase. We simply can't stop and let them off, so we take them for a short test ride before spending quality time with them and sharing our most vulnerable emotions. Unfortunately, not all of the ones we meet pass the first test, so we usually just drop them off at the hospital and wish them well.

Here's what we've learned about relationships with "cougars."

Pros

- No more having to share the wrinkle cream.

- Younger men shovel snow faster.

- Your kids know all of his favorite video games.

- Cubs are more relaxed and interested in sex, when they don't have to live at home anymore.

- Everybody else will think your sex life is "amazing."

- They love to travel, if you can afford it.

Cons

- You've got to turn off YouTube and the game monitor when it's time to have a glass of wine and some milk.

- It's a pain to answer 200 text messages a day rather than one or two phone calls.

- You thought you spent a lot on your hair!

- You're the oldest woman in Aeropostale.

- How many times can you explain it to him?

- He can't talk about movies or books unless they came from Marvel.

- When a buddy asks him, "*How's your old lady?*" It's not because he's a hippie dude.

Catnip

In general, we don't like cats for pets, especially after watching Jackson Galaxy's television show *Cat From Hell*. But after hearing this story, we may change our minds.

Fluffy, a six-year-old Bengal cat, was taking her daily walk around her Newark neighborhood marking her territory, seeing what was new and getting some fresh air before dinner. Halfway down the block, Fluffy climbed up a small crab apple tree to look around and rest for a second.

Within a minute of settling on her favorite branch, Fluffy saw Larry Kowowski walking his two pit bulls, Rocky and Diesel. As expected, as soon as Fluffy caught their eye, they started growling and barking. With drool dripping off both dogs' jowls, Larry took a stick and pushed Fluffy out of the tree.

Bob Elderly, DVM, said he had never seen anything like it. "It was a long day fixing those two dogs. Rocky and Diesel needed close to 300 stitches. Diesel lost an eye and one ear was halfway off"

Larry paused for a minute, and then continued, "And I've never seen a dog with a partially severed tongue. I think I saved enough of it, so Rocky won't have to eat through a straw."

When asked by a reporter about the mayhem, Fluffy's owner, Fred, said, "Fluffy's a good cat. She can be a bit mean sometimes, but overall she's very loving."

The reporter pressed Fred about whether Fluffy had ever done anything like this before.

"No, not really. I make sure I play with her an hour a day to mellow her out before her walk and dinner. She loves to chase the bird toy. She's a hunter, you know."

The reporter asked, "Well, what happened yesterday?"

Fred hesitantly replied, "I forgot to play with her."

Shit Farm

Recently, while we were riding through Michigan, we stopped for a beer in Lodi Township. It's mostly farms with flat roads, Because it's small, there isn't much traffic, so it's a nice ride.

While we were there, one of the regional riding club members told us a story about a farmer and his neighbor that had a property line dispute. As a protest, the farmer scraped up all his cow manure and placed it a couple of feet high along the property line. Naturally, all that stacked shit created a distinctive odor that wafted through the air when the wind blew.

While the idea of a manure fence appealed to us, we can't use it as a strategy in our work because it would take us too long to create enough personal manure to build even a tiny fence. For us, there are more efficient and faster ways to resolve disputes. You could say, we're really good at mediation.

However, it wasn't this particular fence building tactic that caught our interest. It was the word manure. It has an interesting etymology, which might seem strange coming from us.

Mrs. Blanchard, our tenth grade English teacher, encouraged our study of etymology, which looks at the origin of words and how they've changed over time.

One day, she asked us to stay after class to discuss some specific things she thought we could do to improve ourselves. As we were taking notes on everything she said, she used the word incorrigible in a reference to us. We raised our hands and asked her if she could spell that, and maybe use it in sentence to put it into context for us.

She said, "Of course. You two are incorrigible idiots who can't spell shit!" She suggested we hang around for the summer and take a class in etymology which might help us learn to string two words together that make some kind of sense.

At first, we thought etymology might be a cooking class, but thanks to Mrs. Blanchard, we got our first real lessons in understanding and using words. However, she was wrong about us not being able to spell the word "shit." Actually, if she had looked around the school, she would have credited us with using it in several places, both in context and out of context.

With that bit of history, you probably understand why the word manure peaked our interest. According to the Etymology Dictionary, the verb manure appeared around 1400, and came from the French word manynoverer, which essentially means to cultivate the land with one's hands. The noun manure was an offshoot of manynoverer and meant working dung into the soil to make it more fertile.

So what exactly is dung? It's excrement of animals. Humans are animals. We excrete on most good days, but we don't say, "I've got to excrete some dung." We say, "I've got to take a shit."

We see people walking their dogs all the time. Do they walk the dog simply for exercise? No, they walk the dog because they're hoping the dog will drop some manure in any yard but theirs.

If we left our personal manure in someone's front yard, they would be shocked and pissed off, even though they probably use steer manure in their flower beds. Don't worry, we've never done that—at least not yet. We prefer to send ours in a candy box to special friends. It really surprises them!

We were disappointed that locally produced human waste recycling was left out of the Green New Deal. There's nothing in there to encourage people to stop flushing and start fertilizing. Imagine the taste of your home grown tomatoes fertilized with your home grown manure!

Firewood

The DIY Network is being rebranded as the Magnolia Network. One of our favorite shows currently on DIY, Maine Cabin Masters, may not be back. We'll miss it for a lot of reasons.

1. Who knew there were so many uses for garbage cans on the ceiling?

2. Finally, a place where open kitchen shelves and barn doors make sense.

3. Formica countertops never looked so good.

4. All outhouses were two-seaters, so couples could get ready at the same time.

5. The reveal was always exciting for cabin owners because many of them had never been there before.

6. Where else can you see tattoos of snowmobiles?

7. Chip and Joanna Gaines weren't on it.

Big Brother

All 50 states have their own coronavirus restrictions. Most people only know about the standard ones involving public places like restaurants, movies, and grocery stores. But there are other restrictions too.

Texas

To keep the crowds down, all executions will be broadcast live on TV.

With the shortage of ammo, only Republicans can buy bullets now.

The Huntsville Prison Rodeo was called off this year because state officials were worried about the animals catching Covid.

Florida

State officials recommended that all ugly people stay home, which closed most nudist resorts.

Florida's state epidemiologist says if the virus lasts six more months, Florida is going to look a lot younger.

So far, the governor has only shut down the ski resorts.

Georgia

People sitting on their front porch can only wave. No more shouting, singing, or tobacco spitting over the rail.

Shortages are stressing local residents causing an increase in crime. More than 400,000 toothpicks stolen from a factory in Athens have an estimated street value of $3000.

Since the coronavirus outbreak, Georgia has allowed out-of-state people to vote in their elections by requesting a mail-in ballot. There's a limit of five per person.

Alabama

Anyone finding a dead Armadillo on the road can still take it home, but they can't have more than two people over for the barbecue.

All the guys' named Bubba have to declare as Bubba 1, Bubba 2, etc. for use on hospital bracelets. Tobacco chewers are discouraged from spitting into

Dr. Pepper bottles, which are being refilled by the company due to the shortages.

Arkansas

A recent survey found that wearing masks made residents less self-conscious about missing teeth.

Some residents wanted to know the side effects of taking the vaccine while using Oxycontin.

No more bare feet on the dinning room table.

New York

Luxury items are now only sold to people who are likely to live.

Everyone peeing on the sidewalk, or being peed on while on the sidewalk, has to wear a mask.

Criminals are no longer allowed to rob anyone who is sneezing, coughing or who has a fever.

Massachusetts

MIT's school newspaper said recently that MIT

students don't get the virus, they make it. In a survey of MIT's 840 Chinese students, 98 percent agreed.

The owners of the Lizzie Borden Bed & Breakfast are asking guests to stop playing with the axe until it's safe again.

Despite the mysteries of the virus, the single biggest unanswered question in Massachusetts is, "Is Mitt Romney really a Republican?"

Illinois

All bullets must be cleaned daily.

Drive-by shooters must keep their masks on for 20 minutes after the first shot, or until they're two miles away.

Chicago's million-dollar mile is now worth only a $1.98.

Mississippi

People in Mississippi aren't worried about the virus. They figure if you can't spell it, you can't get it.

Anyone sitting on a roof awaiting rescue will be left behind if they're not wearing a mask. If they die, their death will be classified as Covid related.

Visitors going to Pascagoula to see the world's largest shrimp, can't take a bite—unless they're first in line.

Louisiana

Barehanded catfishers shouldn't wear masks because no one can hear them screaming when they catch one.

The Health Department says there is no evidence that strippers on Bourbon Street get lower tips when they wear masks.

Louisiana has adopted the Alabama rule on roadkill Dillos with an exemption for the ones cooked with extra blackened Cajun spices.

Tennessee

Memphis really is singing the blues now.

No Elvis sightings since the outbreak began in March.

All moonshine jars must have a warning label instructing residents to wipe the jar off before drinking the contents.

Kentucky

Open mike night for singing coal miner's daughters is suspended until April.

The feds wanted more testing, so the governor is leaving the bars open to check for the loss of taste.

Kentucky's official dance is clogging. That will be big news in Utah.

Alaska

If two or more hikers encounter a bear, each hiker must run in a different direction. No more running together.

Everybody is already wearing gloves.

Only one person at a time can pet a moose.

North Carolina

All furniture previously built in North Carolina must now be made in China to protect NC workers from the virus.

North Carolina is the home to the first Krispy Kreme store, which has killed as many people as Covid.

There's a limit of two people sitting on the top of an RV, even if it's stopped.

Idaho

Farmers in Idaho asked the coroner to freeze a few dead bodies for hiding in their corn mazes next Halloween.

The fertilizer used on potatoes is free from the virus, which is surprising considering where it comes from!

Contact tracing identified nine hate groups with two members or less.

Colorado

If someone dies of Covid while hiking, Search and Rescue won't look for them for at least one year, but if you can carry them, take them home with you.

Marijuana researchers say stoners living in Colorado haven't heard about Covid, "Yo, dude, virus!"

All those with Covid are encouraged to move to Grand Junction.

Oregon

Tweakers with the virus mildew faster in the rain.

Anarchists rioted on New Year's Eve in Portland. After it was over on New Year's Day, one of them said, "Well, we've only got 365 more to go this year."

If Portland residents want to limit the virus's carbon footprint, they should take light rail to the hospital.

Washington

If Amazon ain't selling it, you just don't need it.

Bellingham tried to move to Canada. It wasn't because of the virus. They just wanted to get away from Seattle.

"An apple a day keeps the doctor away" and so does Covid.

Wyoming

Bar fights are limited to three people or less.

Covid contact requires residents to quarantine in their double-wide for ten days, or during the winter they can sit outside for two hours.

Single selfies only with a buffalo. No more group pictures.

California

Legislators were surprised and a bit confused when they found out that Covid wasn't taxed.

Only one person per tent in camp-grounds. Tents on the sidewalk and in city parks have a limit of ten residents per tent.

The governor closed everything in California except the borders. If they closed those, they couldn't get their drug deliveries.

Utah

The number one question the Health Department gets, "Is Chuck-a-Rama open?"

The governor's office has assigned a task force to negotiate with Kentucky to get clogging back.

The Health Department has issued a warning for this year's buffalo hunt on Antelope Island. Killing a buffalo with piano wire and a pocket knife is especially dangerous this year with most ICU's full.

North Dakota

During the pandemic, out-of-state people aren't allowed to move to North Dakota. Both applicants were turned down in 2020. Better luck next year.

When Dr. Brix visited Bismarck, she said their virus mitigation efforts were the worst she's ever seen. So, the locals quickly put her on a tour of some fracking wells and a coal mine. One official was heard saying, "It's too bad she didn't fall in!"

There's a shortage of rabbit bratwurst this year, so a lot of people are switching to rattlesnake sausage.

South Dakota

Even though the state has the second highest number of Covid cases per 100,000 residents, more people are moving to South Dakota than to North Dakota because the opportunities are better in the South.

South Dakota only has a handful of contact tracers. How many do they need to call everybody?

In South Dakota, a Prius can't make it to the grocery store on a single charge. That's really bad news for liberals.

Oklahoma

In Tulsa, only one preacher at a time on the porch with the morning newspaper.

Because of a shortage of hospital beds, there's a moratorium on hitting tourists who think a bison is just another word for a buffalo.

With only two more wind farms, the Health Department believes they can blow the Covid back to Colorado along with the second hand marijuana smoke.

Kansas

The Kansas City Chiefs asked the NFL to launch an investigation into possible Covid violations by the players' union. Really! Isn't having Patrick Mahomes enough?

Four is the new limit on people hiding in a basement during a tornado. Everyone else should look for an abandoned trailer.

Collecting used floss for the world's largest ball of twine is prohibited, unless it has dried for two days.

Missouri

Lambert's Cafe servers no longer throw rolls to customers. They shoot them over with a sanitized sling shot.

Spitting Skoal through masks is discouraged. Government officials say the stains are hard to get out.

Missouri has the only restaurant built inside a cave. They got the idea from Wuhan; however, bats are no longer allowed to eat there.

Nevada

A lot of people have said, if they hear Wayne Newton sing Dunke Schoen one more time, they'll die. Will those deaths be blamed on the virus?

Pickpockets must wear gloves.

Visitors arriving in Las Vegas with $10,000, or more, must quarantine in a casino for five days and nights before going outside.

Indiana

High schools must have at least eight basketball players on a team, so if two of them get the virus, the team can still win the state championship with the other six.

A casino in French Lick was built on the site of Larry Bird's basketball hoop. While inside the casino, visitors can look at his picture without wearing a mask. His picture is Covid free.

Santa Claus Indiana receives thousands of letters every year addressed simply to Santa Claus. Volunteer residents who previously answered each one are all out with the virus, so the post office stamped them, "Return to Sender—Elves too sick to lick the stamps.,"

Michigan

Governor Gretchen Whitmer shut down Detroit. No one told her it had already shut down ten years earlier.

For contact limiting purposes, beggars at intersections and freeway entrances can have signs that say, "Forget the money. Just give me drugs!"

Michigan abolished the death penalty in 1846. Whitmer reinstated it for gym and restaurant owners who refuse to close. She said, "It's better to kill a few of them than let them get away with disobeying me. We're saving lives here!"

Nebraska

The Health Department issued the three C's for Nebraska residents. Stay out of crowded spaces, no close contact and avoid confined spaces. So no more cornfields after dark? What are teenagers supposed to do?

No more "Aw-shucks" in Nebraska. A simple "Shucks" spreads less virus.

Both light houses in Nebraska are shut down due to the Covid. Hopefully, fog won't cause ships any problem.

Vermont

Vermont has the lowest infection rate per 100,000 people in the US. When Bernie Sanders was asked why, he said, "Communism should be the goal of all Americans."

The state is the largest producer of talc. So apparently Vermont was killing women long before the virus.

Some of the people who died from Covid had traces of Vermont maple syrup in their blood, which likely came from the big stack at I-Hop.

Iowa

Southeast Iowa is the hub of Transcendental Meditation. When Maharishi Mahesh was asked how the virus might impact his school, he responded, "Ohm! Ohm! Ohm!"

Ozzy Osbourne bit the head off of a bat in Des Moines. There are reports the Chinese are considering blaming the Covid outbreak on Ozzy.

The Department of Health issued new guidelines for hay rides. Only one person per bale, or two married people if they sit quietly two feet apart.

Connecticut

Helicopters are delivering the vaccine in Connecticut.

When asked about Covid concerns, residents of Hartford said, "We have insurance."

The Scoville Memorial Library in Salisbury, one of the oldest libraries in America, is still open twenty-four hours a day in case homeless people want to check out a book.

New Hampshire

The New Hampshire Health Department officially listed Vermont as its preferred Covid test site.

When the 981 residents of New Castle tried to social distance on their 0.8 square mile island, four of them fell into the water. Two of them drowned. That accounts for both of their Covid deaths.

There are 234 towns in New Hampshire. About 200 of them have less than 5000 people living there, and very few Covid cases. When the state epidemiologist was asked why there were so few cases in the smaller communities, he said, "They don't have a Walmart."

Maine

Residents of Maine must wear masks, maintain social distancing and wash their hands frequently, even when having sex. The New Hampshire Hotel Association says business is up.

In response to criticism about applying pandemic rules to making love, Governor Mills said , "Maine just needs more federal stimulus."

Rednecks in Georgia panicked when Maine closed the toothpick plant.

Pennsylvania

The Hershey factory is restricting finger licking to individuals and their families only.

Pennsylvania residents were extremely happy to see the first of four trucks carrying the vaccine cross the border. The other three are still somewhere in New Jersey. Luckily, residents can still qualify for priority doses of the vaccine if they meet specific criteria. They have to have $500 in cash, a mask across their eyes and an Uber driver who won't talk about driving them to New Jersey.

No face masks needed under helmets during lawnmower race day.

New Jersey

New Jersey used to be ranked first in the country for longevity—80.7 years. Not anymore.

New Jersey residents have been asking Governor Murphy how much additional unemployment they will get and when. Murphy said, "It's complicated. The Federal government has approved $300 a week extra, but there's the union vig, a little slice for garbage pickup, and of course, there's a small gratuity going back to Trenton."

More cars are stolen in Newark than in any other city. State officials have classified car thieves as essential workers, since they are reducing green house emissions.

Ohio

Ohio residents have to stay home between 10 p.m. and 5 a.m. unless they're picking up take out, grocery shopping or driving around Cleveland hoping to see Lebron James.

Former Cincinnati mayor, Jerry Springer, is thinking of running for national office. When asked why, he said, "I have a lot of experience managing nuts and flakes!"

Ohio murderer, Romell Broom, survived lethal injection 10 years ago and was given a second chance. His new execution date was March of 2022, but he died of coronavirus a week earlier. Just before he bit the dust, he said, "I knew the Chinese would get me."

Virginia

Virginia is the home of Mountain Dew soda. People in Utah think they created it. We guess that's like the clogging thing.

Fundraising for Colonial Williamsburg fell short in 2019, mostly because there were fewer death bequests from old people. They're more optimistic about 2020.

The Dukes of Hazzard Museum ticket sales haven't declined. When asked why, the marketing director for the Museum said, "It's all about a love of history."

West Virginia

Social distancing in West Virginia is 12 feet because a lot of people can spit tobacco 10 feet.

The next roadkill cook-off festival is scheduled for September of 2021. The 2020 festival was canceled because there just weren't enough cars on the road.

People in West Virginia don't buy a lot of prescription drugs. They just make their own.

Hawaii

Tickets to Don Ho impersonator shows are restricted to old people.

Tourists are greeted at the airport with a gift box of wallet wipes. Wallet wipes ensure virus free money removal right down to the last dollar. Mahalo!

At the suggestion of the Hotel Association, all visitors must quarantine for 14 days, in order to save lives, of course.

Maryland

In Baltimore, no murders after 10 p.m. except on the weekends.

Drug dealers are encouraged to sanitize their hands after each sale.

Before March 2020, Maryland used to have 48 residents at least 114 years old. Time for a recount.

Wisconsin

In one of the many lawsuits filed against Governor Tony Evers, he was wrongly referred to as cheddarbrain. That was corrected to cheesehead before filing.

Barbie came from the fictional town of Willows, Wisconsin. In Willows, no one gets the vid, Ken didn't fool around on Barbie, and none of their children had trans identity issues. Tony Evers continues to drive around looking for Willows, so he can shut it down.

The small town of Warrens and its 400 residents host the annual cranberry festival that brings over 100,000 people to town every year. Epidemiologists are studying Warrens to determine why the rate of infection is so high there.

Montana

Only one person per buffalo ride.

Selfies with Kevin Costner look-alikes are strongly discouraged.

The stagecoach from Billings to Bozeman only runs on Saturdays now. You'll have to rent a horse if you need to go sooner.

Delaware

Heated masks are available for the Lewes Polar Bear Plunge.

The Crawfish Boil & Muskrat Stew Festival was moved back to March after the Hard Crab Derby was canceled. People need time to change their plans.

There are 200 times as many chickens in Delaware as there are people. And they're not worried about the bird flu?

Minnesota

After electing Jesse Ventura governor, Al Frankin to the Senate and now Ilhan Omar to Congress, a lot of people think there's already significant brain damage in Minnesota, so the virus won't hurt them.

The mosquitoes ate seven tourists last summer, so the Health Department is advising people to put Deet on their masks.

One in every six residents owns a boat. Refer back to one above.

Rhode Island

So far, all the viruses found in Rhode Island were very small.

The governor asked everyone in Rhode Island to quarantine in Connecticut.

Both restaurants in Rhode Island are closed.

New Mexico

All visitors to New Mexico from high-risk states must quarantine for 14 days. That's like 11 days longer than the average New Mexico vacation.

No more spit in the Adobe blocks.

Los Alamos has a very low rate of coronavirus, which proves radiation kills the virus, roaches and people. Roaches?

South Carolina

During the World Grits Festival, only one contestant at a time in the grits pit.

The Alligator Adventure Park is checking everyone for Covid symptoms to protect the gators in case someone falls in the water.

Visitors to the UFO Welcome Center must wear masks and please, no more "Beam me up, Scotty."

Cancel Me Now

We're fans of country music, so we were surprised to hear this story when we were in Tennessee. Cancel has a different meaning for us than it does on social media.

Ruff McGraw, a rising country music star, was abruptly canceled last Thursday night when in an alcohol fueled interview in Nashville, he said, "Dolly Parton is the best country entertainer ever, but I wish her tits weren't plastic."

McGraw, with two chart climbing songs, *I Torched the Double Wide for Beer Money* and *Last Call, Three Guys and Only One Beer Left*, was immediately blasted on Twitter.

Bob from Kentucky: "How do you know they're plastic? Have you touched them? No, I didn't think so!"

Stella from Arkansas: "Stop thinking about Parton's breasts. Just focus on her music. You know she's more than just a pair of big boobs, you boob."

Linda from Texas: "Dolly's got everything I wish I had, but my husband won't pay for them."

State Rep. (D) John M. Windle, who recently proposed legislation to put a statue of Parton in the Capital, tweeted out' "This brings up some dimensional issues we've got to look at."

McGraw tried to apologize to Dolly and her fans saying, "I didn't mean to disrespect a woman's right to choose her body parts. As soon as I get out of rehab,

I'm going to book a gig at Dollywood and apologize between every song."

While Dolly has talked about her "Virginia Twins" from time to time, her answers have been vague on the enhancement questions. When her 78-year-old husband, Carl, was asked about them, he said "I can't remember seeing them!"

Fresh out of a week of rehab, McGraw wrote his new song, *Don't Recycle My Breasts*, which once again is climbing the charts.

Green Eggs and Ham

Our next discussion is about declining fertility in men. While we don't have this problem, we know that some people may be a bit skeptical of that claim, so we're willing to schedule a sample collection time with them because we're Butch and Louie.

Fertility scientists say that sperm counts in Western countries have dropped by more than fifty percent since 1970, and men's testosterone is declining by one percent a year, With pregnancy rates falling, if the trend continues the population will die off faster than it can be replaced. We're very close to that threshold now, so something needs to be done quickly. One of the proposals under consideration is the Green New Sperm Deal.

- Politicians should stop blaming the low fertility rate on global warming.

- Start a public service campaign to convince young men that women are better than a new video game or iPhone.

- Reduce the paperwork for consensual sex between singles.

- Create new religions that encourage married couples to have at least seven children.

- Give men a one-time $1200 payment to spend on porn subscriptions.

- Supplement sperm made in America with Chinese sperm.

- Ban bacon cheeseburgers.

- Explain to little kids that low sperm count killed the dinosaurs. Now, it's up to them.

- Limit smartphone use to 20 minutes a day so men have time to figure out that women exist outside of fictional bios on dating sites.

Eyewitness Testimony

We pride ourselves on keeping an even demeanor because it's good for business. But not everyone is capable of that. While we were in Spain visiting with some local police, they told us a story about love, jealousy. and a quick temper.

On January 21st, Diego Rodriguez was found dead in his apartment in Valencia, Spain. He was killed by a single gunshot to the head. He died due to mistaken identity.

His American neighbor, Emiliano Perez, told a reporter from Valencia International, "Diego's wife, Gabriella, found some pictures on his computer of him and a beautiful woman having sex in the back of a car. The thought of Diego having an affair sent her into a rage."

"She got her gun and shot Diego in the head while he was sleeping in the bedroom. Everyone in the building heard the shot."

One of the arresting officers noticed something odd in the picture. The woman having sex with Diego looked like a much younger Gabriella.

Confronted with the picture at the police station, Gabriella gasped, then said, "I loved Diego so much. I can't believe I didn't recognize our car!"

French Is in the Air

We were at a local market in Paris looking for some cheese, when we read an odd story in the newspaper.

A French woman who chose to only share her first name, Jolie, got an ugly surprise late one Saturday night when a knocked over candle started a fire in her home.

While the fire department quickly put out the flames, the partially burned home is causing a lot of controversy in the neighborhood. Large gatherings of men, as well as a few women, are standing in front of the home, sometimes for hours. Neighbors have called the police several times to break up the crowds.

Ask about this, Jolie said, " I won't be buying anymore of those *This Smells Like My Vagina* candles from Gwyneth Paltrow."

I Philia

Occasionally, we'll use Wikipedia to check out our current location, or find some history about something we're interested in, like a new gun. We were surprised to find out that only 15 percent of the entries on Wikipedia are posted by women. We surveyed a few people to get their thoughts.

Brian from Little Rock said. "Maybe women get tired of telling men they're wrong!" Brian's wife said, "Or maybe they just get tired of cleaning up men's shit!" (Well, they both like exclamation points!)

Tamika from Birmingham said, "Wikipedia is a racist, sexist website." When asked if she had used Wikipedia, Tamika said, "No, I don't spend any of my time on racist sites run by old white men." (Ah, Tamika, how do you know they're old?)

Mitch from Cedar Rapids said, "That's probably because it sounds like a child porn site." (Mitch it's Wikipedia, as in Encyclopedia, not Wikiphilia.)

My Best Side

Everyday, we use Zoom along with 300 million other people, and it's not just about meetings. It's a practical way to get to know someone when two people can't be in the same location. To improve their experience and make using Zoom fun, Zoom lets users touch-up their skin color, shape their nose, change the background, add masks, put on glasses, or rotate their image. While that works for some people, it's not enough for a lot of users. In response, Zoom has recently expanded its offerings.

First, we're reviewing what's new for men trying to establish a connection on Zoom before meeting someone in person. In part 2, we'll discuss what's new for women. All of these new filters are about being your best self.

1. The Confident Look: Even if you're a dweeb, at least you'll look like a dweeb who knows what he wants and who he is.

2. A Look of Integrity: This is the Mitt Romney special. It's the appearance of never ending virtue signaling with a strong moral character, regardless of one's actual deeds. This is a big one with conmen, politicians and other criminals.

3. A Compassionate Style: With this filter, your potential mate will open up to you. You'll know what's going on in the inside and outside. (What you do with the information about their deepest hopes and dreams is not the responsibility of Zoom, its employees, or its affiliates.)

4. The Emotional Availability Filter: This filter shows sensitivity. It aids in expressing your feelings, but avoids the hangdog, *I'm going to cry*, look.

5. The Sense of Humor Filter: With options like Carrot Top, Jerry Seinfeld, Louis C.K., George Carlin or Bill Maher, this one is a tricky choice. (Bill Cosby is only available if the delusional psychopath filter option was selected.)

For those who can't decide on individual combinations, Zoom has developed the single, all encompassing *Bad Boy* image.

1. Client Eastwood: snarling lipped "Make My Day" filter.

2. Ice-T: the "Let's Get Real" filter.

3. Elon Musk: boyish "Samurai Mentality" filter.

4. Bruce Springsteen: steel mill "Rocker Dude" (sober version) filter.

5. Wayne Newton: "Dunkershane, Dunka Shane, Danke Schoen" filter—well, one of those. It's for the softer side of Bad Boy.

As an added tweak, users can play *Born to be Wild* in the background while chatting. That really sets a mood.

Instead of the Bad Boy filter, you can choose the *I'm Intellectually Appealing* filter. It comes with multiple options also.

1. Will Hunting (Matt Damon version): This one is for potential partners who prefer a regular down- to-earth janitor who went to MIT and cleaned it.

2. Steven Hawking: Well, obviously this one attracts the caretaker types.

3. Warren Buffet: Some people like a really, really rich guy in a cheap suit near death.

Finally, hidden away at the bottom of the menu is the *Born Loser* filter. This is a special option for those that just can't make any of the other filters work. If you can overlook previous addictions, personality disorders, cheating bitches (or bastards), and mousy people who can't make a decision for themselves, this may be the one that gets you the partner of your dreams.

_____ ____

My Best Side Part 2

In part 2 of what's new in Zoom filters, we're reviewing a few of the ones for women. Like those for men, these aren't look adjusters; they're persona enhancers.

1. Perfect mother: This one is powerful when talking to a potential family partner. It says I can home school four kids, keep a perfect house, write five books and the only thing I like better than cooking—is sex.

2. The Muse: They'll want you so bad it hurts, and because of your elusive nature they will chase you everyday hoping for just one more encounter. They won't care about kids, cooking or an orderly home because their brains will be like Jell-O.

3. The Confident One: Your IQ stands out. You are clearly saying, "I want you, but I don't need you."

4. Financially Independent: This one says money won't be an issue in your relationship because you can take care of yourself. However, you won't make your partner feel inferior about lagging financially, only loved and adored for who they are.

5. Balanced Emotional Intelligence: This one says you're an even keel girl who not only relates to other's emotions but can clearly communicate and share her feelings. You're cool-headed and warm at the same time.

6. $2000/hr Escort: This is the Vassar grad with the big bucks wardrobe, perfect social skills and an amazing come-hither personality. This is for the partner who doesn't need attention often, just on specific occasions.

In addition to these general persona generators, Zoom has added a few comprehensive packages that combine a little physical touchup with some persona tweaks.

1. Jennifer Aniston: Elusive, hot, ages great and says "I'm really good, if you can get me."

2. Tina Fey: Nothing says fun to be with more—amusing, attractive, intelligent, and yet, so approachable.

3. Michelle Obama: Make everybody think you've got the "it."

4. Kylie Jenner: With an open checkbook ready to play, this filter attracts those who don't need

5. much attention, look good in formal wear, or hip casual clothes, and have expensive tastes.

6. Madonna: This one is for someone who likes an older partner, a high heel shoe in their chest at least a couple of times a week and who doesn't mind being told what to do.

7. Rosanne Barr: Some people just need daily abuse to feel good about themselves.

8. Scarlett Johansson: Those that live in the moment can't resist the steamy "lick all the chocolate off me" seduction.

And these are only a few of the possibilities. Zoom is constantly refining its options, but please don't ignore the disclaimers. Zoom clearly states that maintaining these personas in person is challenging, and that the failure to do so could lead to unexpected consequences.

It's Cold Outside

We love spending time with our fellow bikers in New York. It's always a wild ride there.

Since 2013, New York City's Time Square has been the home to a group of female panhandlers called Desnudas, which is Spanish for naked. Covered in body paint, these topless female performers will join visitors in selfies for a small gratuity.

While not officially recognized by the Bureau of Labor Statistics, Desnudas performers are in a rapidly growing, high-paid profession. Many of the ladies, who dare to go bare, make more than $2000 a week. (Of course, the paint job affects the cash flow.) So, let's see if this line of work is right for you or your daughters?

Pros

It really cuts down on the laundry bills.

No eye strain from looking at a computer screen all day long.

It's a patriotic use for their extra red, white, and blue paint.

They only need a small bag to store their personal items in when they get arrested.

Out of tip money? No problem. They know the location of every ATM.

It's easy to get a cab.

Cons

They're still paying off the plastic surgery bill.

Putting the paint on thicker doesn't help when it's cold.

If they see a kid running at them hollering, "Mommy, Mommy!" that's not good.

Taking the subway home is tricky. They don't have any pockets for tokens.

Describing their profession on dating websites takes careful wording.

They must learn to sing *Wind Beneath My— Wings?*

Stay for Dinner

DNA from a partially eaten sausage left behind after a robbery got a German burglar caught. But, that isn't the first time that DNA from food has identified a bad guy. In 2002, the cops thawed out a piece of frozen fried chicken from 1993 to get DNA. They used it to apprehend the guy responsible for multiple murders at a fast-food restaurant.

This is one reason why we're very careful to cleanup, regardless of what we're doing. In fact, some of our friends think we're a bit obsessive about our leave nothing behind rule. Well, maybe, but it's good for the environment and us. What about you?

"When you're committing a felony, it's not the time to have dinner," said Richard from Wyoming. (That's true, Richard, but more people are eating out because they're just too busy to cook.)

Laurel from Mississippi said, "Criminals are just dumb!" (You have a point, Laurel. Some of them are. However, white collar criminals like a good bottle of wine with their chicken.)

"DNA is amazing. Is there anything the cops can't get DNA off of?" asked Charles from Texas. (Using DNA to solve crimes, Charles, is providing a lot more family information for genealogy enthusiasts.)

"It's hard to believe someone can eat while killing another person," said Gayle from California. (Psychopaths can multi-task, Gayle.)

Walk in My Shoes

Oliver McCrindle of Batemans Bay, Australia, noticed his dog, Bondi, was limping and holding up one paw whenever they went for a walk. At home, Bondi seemed okay, and he didn't have any signs of pain when McCrindle stroked his paw.

However, concerned that Bondi might have a serious medical issue, McCrindle took him to the vet.

Chris Bucks, DVM, examined Bondi and ran numerous tests, including x-rays and a CAT scan. After completing over $600 worth of tests, Bucks told McCrindle, "There's nothing medically wrong with Bondi. But I noticed you have a cane."

"Yes," McCrindle said. "I sprained my ankle a week ago and have to use the cane to walk. Even with the cane, I still limp a bit."

Bucks sort of chuckled and explained, "I think Bondi has developed a sympathetic limp to match yours. It's unusual, but it happens."

McCrindle didn't respond right away as he absorbed the news. Finally, he said, "Well, I guess it's a good thing Bondi didn't see the wife and I having sex!"

Call of Nature

While we were in Venice Beach recently, we found out that during the next few years, several cities in California are banning natural gas as an energy source in new homes. However, the small town of Idlewhil is taking things one step further. Beginning in 2025, no more indoor bathrooms. Construction of new homes must include an outhouse.

Bob Kidding, the Zoning Department head, said, "Bathrooms waste a lot of water and energy, and all that waste has to be processed, which uses even more resources. So we're going back to a time when things were simpler and less costly."

The exact plans for implementing the outhouse concept are somewhat sketchy. Currently, one idea is to build each new home with an outdoor potty that has a removable catch basin for holding one to two weeks of waste for a family of four. Once the basin is full, the family will load it up in their car and drop it off at an assigned space in a wooded area 10 miles outside of town.

A hundred years ago when cabins sat on a lot of land, homeowners simply moved their latrine to a new spot on their property. John Handolman, the mayor, said, "With the smaller lots we have now, there's just no place to move the potting shed," he said laughing. "So we'll keep the shed and move the potting!"

The Forestry Department at a nearby university has endorsed the idea because they believe it provides a rich natural source of fertilizer for the trees and plants that live in the woodlands.

So far, more than 80 residents have inquired about permits for the new "brown" building concept.

Matt Liberalman said, "This sounds like a really workable idea that will help the climate, which is something we really want to do." He continued, "And it will give us more time for outdoor activities with the kids. It's a real win, win."

Handolman said, "We think once the rest of the country sees what we're doing here, the idea will spread. It may take a few more tweaks to get it to work in larger cities, but San Francisco and L.A. already have experience with outdoor bathrooms, so it won't take them long to adapt."

Chew Toys

We don't have any pets, at least not permanent ones. We tried stuffing a couple of them in our saddlebags, but it didn't work out. So now, we'll pick up a temporary one if we're going to be hanging around somewhere for more than a few days.

Last year, pet owners spent $95.7 billion on their pets with $29.3 billion on vet bills and $36.9 billion on food, and that doesn't include the wine. That's a lot of money, but it's easy to see where it goes when pet stores in Carmel, California charge $50,000 for a diamond encrusted dog collar that also comes with a Glock 19 and a dog-napping prevention class.

Thirty years ago, if Fido came down with cancer, one Sunday afternoon Dad would put him in the back of the station wagon and drive off as everybody waved good bye. Everyone knew Fido was going to a better place.

Now, it's not uncommon for pet owners to spend $10,000 or more on chemo hoping to keep Fido peeing in his diaper for another year. Most psychologists think this kind of expense is harmless as long as it doesn't take away from other financial obligations like feeding the kids. However, they also point out that veterinarians have to feed their kids too, and not all of them get a TV show on the Animal Planet network.

Beyond new toys, gourmet food, and the best medical care, pet owners are now using pet psychologists. The Psychology School Guide states that a master's degree is the minimum educational requirement for pet counseling, but most animal therapists have figured out all they need is a card that says they talk to animals for $120 an hour. Apparently, that's adequate for most pet owners.

Counselors like Betty from Colorado are in big demand by both pet owners and ranchers. In a recent visit to one ranch, a steer told her he was upset that the male pig had a female companion, and he didn't. Her recommendation: set up play dates with a nearby rancher that has lonely cows. Unfortunately, Betty is currently charged with pimping.

Another pet psychic, Linda, explained to the owners of Lucy, the family Lab, "Lucy gets bored when everyone stares at their phones. Lucy told me she's thinking, *You're going to do that again! Let's go outside instead.*"

Based on her conversations with Lucy and other dogs, Linda is working with Inward Hound on developing a new chew toy that looks exactly like a cell phone. Dogs can chew it and bury it in the backyard to send a message to their owners. The new toy is expected to relieve canine stress and save a few iPhones.

A Better World Through Plastics

While we were hosting some guests from Japan during an educational event at our local riding club, they told us a few stories. This one was our favorite.

Senji Nakajim grew tired of regular relationships with women, so he bought a $6000 lifelike silicone sex doll. The 63-year-old Japanese businessman admits that after three months of spending time together, he's in love with Himari.

He sits with her at the dinner table, he shops with her, he bathes her, he sleeps next to her, and he takes her for walks by pushing her in a wheelchair. And yes, they have sex, but Senji is very considerate of Himari's feelings and moods.

"For me, she is more than a doll." said Senji. "She needs help with a lot of things, but she is my perfect partner. She supports me 100 percent and enriches my life."

Senji enjoys buying Himari clothes, wigs and even jewelry. He says she has favorite outfits, but each new one brings excitement and sometimes a mood change.

"Her personality fits me well," Senji said. "We enjoy the same TV shows, restaurants, and movies."

Despite what looks like a very successful and compatible relationship, Senji's friends encouraged him to get counseling. They worried he was slowly losing perspective.

At first, Senji disagreed, but a few months ago, he decided to spend time talking to Dr. Akito Kobayashi, a local psychiatrist.

Once a week, Senji takes Dr. Kobayashi out of the closet, and the two of them sit in the living room discussing everything from work to Senji's love life.

Senji says that his friends were right. "Dr. Kobayashi has helped me maintain balance. He's also given me suggestions on managing relationship issues with Himari. I'm very happy to have both of them in my life."

Curbside Service

While looking into the vaccine before getting our shots, we learned a few things that aren't mentioned by TV doctors.

1. It's better to get your vaccination in a drive-thru location, so you can't hear the people in front of you screaming.

2. If you don't trust the vaccine, ask the nurse to let you smell it and taste it before taking the shot.

3. Expired vaccine looks just like brand new vaccine.

4. Don't worry, your body loves foreign artificial crap being forced into it.

5. You'll get a reminder card to schedule your second dose, just in case the first dose causes brain damage.

6. No matter where you get your first shot, it's going to look like a super spreader party, so you better hope this stuff works fast.

7. If you get your shot at Walmart, make sure the vial says *Made in America.*

8. You can get a Fauci band-aid.

9. If you're wondering why the nurse has pliers on the table, that's just in case the needle breaks off in your arm.

A Different Cord

We told you about our love of Girl Scout cookies, and we're not the only ones that like a good tasting cookie once in a while.

In Karlsruhe Germany, a court recently ruled that an online cookie company had to stop selling their cookies made with sawdust. Since 2004, the company has used sawdust in their cookie dough and has never received a complaint.

The owner argued in court that his sawdust was micro-biologically sound, and it was a source of fiber. In fact, he had even disclosed it as an ingredient on the label along with raisins and flour. His sawdust supplier testified in court that the sawdust was actually a vegetable product. But the court ruled against him anyway. He knew this would disappoint his customers.

Annike eats the cookies weekly and was surprised to hear there was sawdust in them. He said, "Well, that explains why I've had an urge to put furniture polish on my legs."

Asked if she had read the label and noticed the sawdust listed with the other ingredients. "Yes," Margarethe said, "but eating them kept me really regular. Every morning I shit a couple of nice logs!"

Kurt told one reporter that, "I tried the new cookies without the sawdust, but I kept wanting to chew on a toothpick all day."

Somebody's Got to Do It

It's an unfortunate part of our lifestyle, but we do have to interact with Medical Examiners from time to time. We always ask them, "Got any new stiffs, Doc?"

Felix Barski, MD, said, "I really like working with people. For me, that's a big plus. The downside is I see a lot of the same stuff everyday. Gunshot wounds, stabbings—the usual. Give me a good beating, or maybe a crispy critter from a house fire, just to break things up."

Brenda Smalls, MD, told us, "When I was doing my rotations in medical school, I hated listening to all my patient's personal bullshit. Now, my patients never say a word. Of course, that means I don't have anybody to talk to either. Well, at least no one who answers me back." Brenda smiled, "Yet!"

Samuel Berg, MD, said, "I like taking things apart and putting them back together." He laughed, "It's like rebuilding a carburetor, you don't want to have any extra parts laying on the table when you're done. Of course, I don't like handling all the squishy stuff."

If one of your kids is considering a career as an Influencer, DJ, YouTube star, or gamer, have them talk to their guidance counselor about careers as a Medical Examiner. We never met a Medical Examiner still living in their parent's basement.

As an alternative, you could hire us as life coaches for your kids. We'll help them find a new way of looking at things—really fast.

Turn Out the Lights

As doctors bring more patients back from death, near death memories are increasing. While many near death experiences may sound similar, they are definitely not identical. In our travels, we've met a few people who have died and then returned, so we asked them to tell us what it was like.

Robert Earl from Mississippi said, "I died after a bar fight. I remember floating above the bar watching everyone. I even saw my wife dancing with another man, and I wasn't even mad." Robert Earl came back in the emergency room after his heart was shocked. He looked at the doctor and asked. "Where's that bitch?"

Holly, who grew up on a farm, is from Wisconsin. As a supporter of the Packers, she's proud to be called a "Cheesehead." She explained she crashed her car while delivering pizzas. After a few minutes, she felt herself slipping away. She remembers being very calm as the ENT's tried to get her back. She recalls smiling and feeling good. Ask about what she saw while she was "dead," she said, "Dairy Cows!"

Shanice, from North Carolina, collapsed while she was singing in the choir. She briefly regained consciousness, and then was gone again. Out for nearly 30 minutes, her doctors were about to give up when she gasped for breath and opened her eyes. As she regained her senses, she seemed disappointed to be back. Shanice told us she wasn't disappointed that she couldn't stay in heaven. She said, "I was on the finals of the Voice."

It Ain't Over Till It's Over

We try to avoid discussing politics. It's a divisive subject. It's like when you ask someone if you can dance with their old lady (Old lady, a loyal female companion who knows the difference between a knucklehead and a panhead.) We met Les and Hollis when we stopped to have a beer in Alabama.

In October, they decided to make a $100 bet on who would win the presidential election.

"Lester and I been friends since we was kids, but we dudn't agree on everything, including if Mr. Trump should be president," said Hollis.

Hollis continued, "Well, at the end of November I told Les to pay up since Trump lost, but Les said it wudn't over."

"By the middle of January, I was fixing to get mad at Les no matter how long we been friends. I told him I wud shoot him for the $100 because a debt is a debt, but Les just kept sayin it wudn't over."

"Finally, our friend, Aldon, said we should just make it double or nuttin on the 2024 election because dat made more bidness sense than shooting Les. So Les and I shook on it, and we're drinkin buddies again —at least for four mo years! "

Look It Up

This year, in October, as the world celebrates Dictionary Day, there's one two-word phrase that consistently defies definition. It has been that way since the publication of Webster's original 1828 dictionary. Those two words are *fair share*.

William Littleton, a Merriam lexicographer, explained, "The debate over the meaning of *fair share* has gone on for close to 200 years. Some of the really old lexicographers tell stories of *fair share* debates where people wound up throwing pencils, erasers and a Ding Dong or two at each other." He chuckles a bit, "In the world of lexicography, that's really something since most of us are dorks."

In the 1800's, *fair share* concerned property like chickens, pigs and horses. Should someone who won two pigs and a horse in the colonial lottery have to give one pig to the government to feed the president, or should they be allowed to trade one pig for 15 chickens and turnover five of those chickens instead? Of course, there was the question of should a lottery winner contribute more to the federal stew pot than say someone who worked his farm for 20 years to get the pig and the horse.

Even in today's common usage, the meaning of *fair share* varies by age, political party and those contemplating a permanent life on welfare. Gen Z's tend to believe that *fair share* means everything older people have, but not my stuff. Millennials divide upon this issue between those who have an established career and earn their money, and those still living at home with their parents.

"Watching members of Congress argue whenever a discussion of *fair share* comes up," says Frank Armstead, a senior thinker at the Boston Conservative Think Tank, "tells us we aren't even close to a definition yet."

"But," he continued, "in Karl Marx's Communist Manifesto, it says right on page one that *fair share* means taking ninety percent of everything every worker earns and giving it to government officials and their friends. So Karl Marx had a clear vision of what a *fair share* should be."

With more junior high 10- and 11-year-olds checking out copies of Marx's Manifesto from the school library, we may be getting closer to establishing what a *fair share* is. That's probably why a few members of Congress want to drop the voting age to 13.

Very Complex

We've all heard the term military-industrial complex used by politicians and the news media. But very few people really understand what that is. After Vietnam, we understood it really well, so here's our take.

Military: These are the people who use really, really big bullets—sometimes lots of them.

Industrial Complex: These are the people who make the really, really big bullets for the military.

Ammo: That's shorthand for every bullet from the small ones to the big ones. It also includes ammo accessory items like ships, planes and missiles. Of course, shipping and handling are included with every order.

Military Promotions: These are almost always given to the military people who order lots and lots of ammo for shooting at people with smaller ammo.

Industrial Complex Promotions: These usually go to the people who sell lots and lots of ammo to the military people after buying them dinner, drinks and placing them in compromising situations.

Best Used By Date: All ammo has a best used by date stamped on it. That date coincides with the industrial complex's employee performance reviews for pay raises and bonuses. Then there's the expiration date. That's the last day the ammo is guaranteed to work reliably before politicians have to run for re-election. And, finally, there's the turn-to-shit date. On the turn-to-shit date, the ammo starts leaking toxins and exploding in its boxes. Then it costs lots and lots of money to put it in the garbage.

War Machine: This is a figurative term since it's not actually a machine but a group of politicians and lobbyists who insist that all the ammo must be used before it expires. Letting the ammo expire means lower bonuses, smaller salary increases and fewer promotions.

Think Tank: This is a place where Ivy League liberal arts graduates work. Sometimes, retired military generals work there too because they're good at dinner and drinks and explaining why there is never enough ammo. They really like the new stuff with WiFi.

CIA: This is the government version of a think tank; however, the CIA can only afford liberal arts graduates from state universities. Because they don't have the persuasive powers or expense accounts of the Ivy League graduates, they have to use recorded conversations, photographs and fake stuff created on a computer to identify safe places run by bad people that are good disposal sites for the ammo.

The Pentagon: Almost everyone at the Pentagon is an ammo counter. A few employees circle the CIA disposal sites on a map, which leaves a couple of senior managers available for dinner, drinks and blackmail. And there are two generals, who are ready for retirement, who stay prepared to testify at Congressional hearings on ammo issues.

GAO: This is the government accounting office. One of their jobs is to count the money the military spends on ammo. They reconcile receipts for travel, dinners and compromising situations against the bills from the industrial complex. From millions of line-item entries since 1776, they've concluded that almost no ammo has expired because it was used in wars 228 out of the last 245 years,

US Citizen: These are the co-signers on the government loans used to pay for the industrial complex bonuses, and the women the generals love spending time with. There must be some benefit to co-signing these loans. The GAO is still reviewing that question.

Recent College Graduate: These are young people who think the military industrial complex is Google's office campus. They're in for a surprise.

Lock Them Up!

We know a lot of politicians from working at rock concerts, or from doing our specialized type of DoorDash brown bag delivery. And, we know lots of psychopaths too, so we compared them for you.

- Psychopaths don't feel any guilt if they lie to you or mislead you to get what they want. Politicians are very mindful of the truth and would never lie or mislead.

- Psychopaths watch those around them, so they fit in to maintain their cover. Politicians never base their actions on what those around them are doing. They are open and have no cover to maintain.

- Psychopaths have a poor inner sense of right and wrong. Politicians have a very strong inner sense of right and wrong, and they only do what's right.

- Psychopaths lack empathy. They don't understand how others feel, and they don't care. They see others as objects usable for their own benefit. Politicians feel everyone's pain and have a total understanding of how others feel. That's all they care about.

- Psychopaths use manipulation and reckless behavior to get what they want. Politicians never manipulate people simply to get what they want.

- Psychopaths frequently appear to be perfectly normal, ambitious people climbing the upward ladder. Politicians are only concerned about doing what's best for the voters, not getting ahead.

- Psychopaths are often charming, intelligent, reflect others emotions, and pretend to be interested in them. Politicians are really interested in us. Just ask them.

- Psychopaths are good actors. Politicians never put on an act. They're sincere, genuine people. They would never manipulate others for personal gain.

- Psychopaths are calculating. They plan their moves and carry out the plan to accomplish their goals. Politicians are not calculating. What you see is what you get.

- Psychopaths will take out anyone or anything that is in the way of whatever they're after. They'll destroy reputations, cost people their jobs or paint others with an ugly broad brush

- to move them aside. Politicians respect others; even those that disagree with them.

Clothing Optional

Don't forget that July 14th is National Nude Day. While it's not recognized as an official holiday, it is a chance to be free of clothes for a few hours. Unlike Spain, which has its nudity rights in its constitution, laws in the US vary from state-to-state. If you want to celebrate National Nude Day with us, you need to know the rules, along with a few tips.

Texas: Hippie Hollow Park in Austin is clothing optional, but all the hippie's moved and got jobs.

Florida: Don't forget to put your sunscreen in between all the wrinkles.

Georgia: Naked above the waist appears to be okay, but they're still trying to figure out the meaning of lewd. So are we.

Alabama: It isn't even legal to post pictures of naked people, unless you include an address so the police can arrest them.

Arkansas: It's not legal to advertise or publicly support getting naked. Not even on Craigslist!

New York: Nudity is allowed all year long in front of your apartment windows.

Massachusetts: If you have a Harvard tattoo, please skip Nude Day.

Illinois: Nudity is permitted everywhere except in front of Oprah's house.

Mississippi: Going outside in your underwear to get the mail doesn't count.

Louisiana: No nudity except at Mardi Gras. We're there!

Tennessee: If you think you saw Elvis nude, just go on over to the hospital.

Kentucky: Be careful, moonshine stills get hot.

Alaska: Public nudity is allowed only in the winter and is restricted to the outdoors.

North Carolina: No nudity at NASCAR races until the race is over to prevent driver distraction.

Idaho: Ballet dancers can dance in the nude, but you can't, unless you're at one of the five hot springs in Idaho.

Colorado: There are a lot of places to get naked in Colorado, but not in front of the weed store.

Oregon: Nudity at the hot springs is okay all the time. And nudity around a warm puddle larger than 12 inches is okay after a night of looting, rioting or anarchy.

Washington: Some cities allow you to be nude anywhere anytime as long as you're not making others uncomfortable. What?

Wyoming: Cowboy hats and boots are optional after 4 pm, if you're not wearing anything else.

California: California has its naked bike ride day, which equals: fill up the emergency room day.

Utah: Are you kidding; don't even ask!

North Dakota: When free climbing nude, you must tape your ID to your ass.

South Dakota: It's okay to get naked in 99.9 percent of South Dakota. The tumbleweed doesn't care.

Oklahoma: Nudity isn't legal in Oklahoma, unless you can outrun the cops and a preacher waving a Bible.

Kansas: Nudity is okay in Kansas as long as you walk fast. Wow! Who would have guessed?

Missouri: This place doesn't even allow breastfeeding in public, so imagine how outraged they would be if you put the baby down.

Nevada: With a million strip clubs in Nevada, you would think you could get naked in one of them.

Indiana: Standing naked in your front yard will get you busted. What about around back?

Michigan: Take off your clothes at one of Michigan's five nudist resorts, or when ice sailing on Lake Michigan.

Nebraska: You can't even go swimming in your own backyard pool without a suit and tie.

Vermont: No marching naked Bernie Bros carrying signs demanding free healthcare and higher taxes.

Iowa: Somewhere between Cedar Rapids and Iowa City there's a place known as Bare Butt Hill. What map is that one on?

Connecticut: Two campsites don't require clothes. But the view from the back of the mansion isn't great.

New Hampshire: There's no state law against going topless, but that's as far south as it goes.

Maine: No lobster fishing in the nude. Too many embarrassing injuries.

Pennsylvania: This place even has laws against sexting. What's next?

New Jersey: Nudity is okay as long as you buy a permit and pay the nude tax.

Ohio: Nude fishing is okay on the Ohio River as long as no one in Kentucky can see you.

Virginia: It's hard to believe, but these guys tried to put someone in jail for being naked in their house. And Virginia is for lovers?

West Virginia: The one clothing optional resort burned to the ground and all the clothes with it.

Hawaii: Take half off everywhere and the rest at private beaches.

Maryland: Naked drive-by shootings are not allowed.

Wisconsin: Eating cheese naked is okay here.

Montana: Nude buffalo hunting is discouraged.

Delaware: This is a tight-assed state. Flashing your butt in public is illegal.

Minnesota: Ten thousand lakes and only one cop.

Rhode Island: There's no where to run, if you're caught.

New Mexico: Stick to Santa Fe with lots of old hippie's that get it.

South Carolina: If you see a naked banjo player, run!

Index

Ammo	47,104-106
Ass	14,26.113
Bad Boys	Butch & Louie
Basement	27,98
Bill Cosby	79
Born Loser	80
Breast	7,8,9, 71,72
Cat	Really! 41,88
Caulk	8
Covid	This book is vaccinated!
Dead	16,31,48,75,99
Dolly Parton	8,71
Jail	27,113
Jennifer Aniston	83
Jerry Seinfeld	79
Naked	15,85,110-113
Nude	110-113
Possum	16
Psychopath	79,87,107-109
Silicone	7,8,9,93
Tits	8,9,71
Vagina	76

Butch & Louie Bio

Who are Butch and Louie?

Societally unacceptable—with no plans to change!

Is that it?

We write vignettes about people, places and life events as seen through our bad boy eyes.

Here are a few things other people have said about us. Maybe that will provide you a window into our non-redemptive asses.

Sargent Bernard Walsh, "Butch and Louie are two witty guys. They make me laugh every time I have to talk to them."

Detective Mannie Lopez, "These guys are fun to be with. I never leave the room without a smile."

Bail Bondsman Martie McGee, "Butch and Louie always have a funny story to tell. I love it when they come in."

Pastor Michael Washington, "I love being around these dirty a'holes."

Marta, Professional Reviewer "You both clearly have a wicked sense of humor and an interesting take on life and this really shines through in your book, making it an interesting read".

Thanks Marta.

Did you guys really write this book and why?

Or you asking if we can right? (Mrs. Blanchard, our 10th grade English teacher, used to ask the same question. She was key to our early graduation.)

Of course, we wrote it. Sometimes, when we're having a bad day, like right after an interrogation, we need a few good laughs to make the day go better. We thought you could use some too.

Do you guys really ride Harleys?

Panhead humorists don't ride bicycles!

Have you two ever been in prison?

Well, that depends on what you mean by "in." We do make deliveries to prisons on occasion.

A better question might be, have you guys ever been convicted of anything?

No—at least not yet! Despite what Mrs. Blanchard thought, we're smarter than we look. We should put that on a tat!

Is there anything else you want to tell us?

Experience Panhead humor firsthand. Saddle up; it's time to ride.

Watch for Facebook promotions and posts to get free copies of Butch & Louie's books. And don't forget to keep us happy with good reviews on Amazon and Barnes and Noble, so we won't park in front of your house. It's disruptive!

Google: Facebook Butch & Louie It's that simple!

Made in the USA
Monee, IL
30 May 2021